seasons of letting go

By Frances Ruthe Figart

ISBN-10: 0-9980116-0-6
ISBN-13: 78-0-9980116-0-8

Book design and layout by Trish Griffin Noe
Cover photo by Joye Ardyn Durham

For Mary and Joe

Contents

Introduction

For several years in the late 2000s, I lived alternately in Costa Rica and New Brunswick, Canada, as the partner of a kayak tour operator I met through my work in ecotourism. Feeling that I'd found the love of my life and the most exciting places on earth, I was swept up in an international experience full of adventure and romance.

From the Bay of Fundy's record-breaking tides to the lush tropical forests of the Nicoya Peninsula, I lived each day immersed in the beauty of the ocean environment. I relished gorgeous sunrises and sunsets, thrilled to rare wildlife sightings and fully embraced my marketing role in support of sustainable travel. To say there was never a dull moment would be putting it lightly.

Back in the States, my mother was becoming weakened by the combination of a leaky heart valve and a chest wall damaged years before by breast cancer, a radical mastectomy and cobalt radiation. Faced with a heartbreaking decision, I ultimately traded my exotic life for what I expected would be a mundane existence: living with my mom in my old hometown of Winchester, Kentucky.

But soon I would find myself navigating a terrain rougher than any the adventure travel realm could offer. Being around to lend a hand morphed into a new role for which I was wholly unprepared: caregiver. I started a blog so that I would not lose touch with my writing or my network of friends and colleagues. The essays that follow formed the core of that blog and chronicle my journey through the most challenging and rewarding experience of my life.

I

seasons of letting go

"Hydrangeas on the Porch" illustration by Linda Santell

spring

Scrabble in the dark with Annie

"So much of our anguish is created when we are in resistance. So much relief, release, and change are possible when we accept, simply accept." ~MELODY BEATTIE

Last September, I started a new job. I didn't expect to get it; I didn't even apply. It's not 9–5; I'm on the clock for all three shifts, every day, 24/7. It's hard, but it's rewarding. And, thankfully, there are a lot of perks.

I'm caring for my mom, at home, by myself. She has congestive heart failure. Without going into medical details, what I am doing on the physical level is kind of like the first year with a newborn—meals every couple of hours, up several times during the night—except that in this case, what everyone is "looking forward to" is not growing up, but transitioning out of this life.

Every caregiving situation is different, with a myriad of complex nuances and ups and downs specific to the patient and the family; in our case, I am the only child, so all of the responsibility to meet my mom's needs and communicate them to others rests with me. "The family caregiver is the backbone of our broken health-care system," writes Gail Sheehy in her book *Passages in Caregiving*. We do it out of love, we do it because our parents did it for us, but make no mistake, it *is* work and it *is* a job.

Social acquaintances see me these days and say, "Wow, you look so tired. Don't you have

"There are only two ways to live your life. One is as though nothing is a miracle. The other is as though everything is." ~ALBERT EINSTEIN

Hospice? And didn't you hire someone to help you?" As if these make everything peachy keen.

Having Hospice is great; it allows me to keep Mom at home where she wants to be and make quick decisions about managing her care. A nurse visits once a week; someone can come if we have a crisis; most of Mom's meds and other equipment like oxygen are provided. But Hospice does not physically help someone like me take care of an elderly person at home on a day-to-day basis. If I want help—with cleaning, with cooking, with everything!—that part is up to me to figure out.

Mom and I did hire a wonderful caregiving assistant a few months ago, and that does allow me to take some vital worry-free breaks. But even families who are well off are hard put to have people working round-the-clock in their homes; we have our caregiver between 12 and 24 hours a week, which is only a fraction of the time I'm on duty. So ultimately, I still have the three-shift job that has been compared to that of a combat soldier in terms of the amount of cortisol produced by the adrenal gland to cope with the stress of a typical day.

I do get to take naps whenever I can squeeze them in. They are usually cut much shorter than I would want—when I hear my mom stirring on the baby monitor—but they are a lifesaver. On "Pauladays," I may get to take a walk before grocery shopping. About once a month, I try to get away for a weekend, which requires coordinating several sitters; and all such plans are subject to change if Mom is feeling especially bad. Sometimes by the time I get a break, I'm way too tired to enjoy a long hike or a concert; I just need rest.

Before taking on this role, I was an "adventurer." I lived to travel and have new experiences in exotic natural settings. Now, I am learning to see the adventures, even the miracles, unfolding before me right where I am. Like the amazing hydrangeas in our garden this year. I have given away at least a dozen arrangements of them, and every time I cut one, three more grow back in its place. Or the amazing two-week visitation to our yard of a group of migrating Rose-breasted Grosbeaks earlier this spring. What a gift it was for my mother to be able to sit on our screened-in back porch and enjoy these special birds. These are glorious adventures for me!

In the few years leading up to this acute stage of Mom's illness, I was always subjected when visiting her to the incessant Cincinnati Red's baseball games blaring at me over her radio. I resisted learning about the game and tolerated the noise without paying much attention to Mom's commentary about her favorite sport. I took her to a game once a few years back, and I admit it was slightly more interesting to see the action live. When Mom got really sick last fall, I decided she needed to be able to see all the Reds games this year on television. We bought a package of some 200 cable channels just to get the one: Fox Sports Ohio. And now, guess who's watching and cheering on the team every night right along with Ruthe, even though she can't stay up for a whole game these days. I like to think it's no accident they are ranked first in their division this year.

Rose-breasted Grosbeak photo by Warren Lynn

Back about November, a friend turned me on to Words With Friends, an online version of Scrabble I can play on my iPhone with Facebook friends. This became a wonderful stress reliever, especially while sitting up with mom during difficulties in the night. I soon found myself playing lots of games with Annie, a friend from high school that I never got to know very well. We made a good match, enjoying some very close games. When we started chatting, I learned that she, too, was caregiving for her mother, who had the same disease as mine. Like me, Annie found the game a great diversion. We had lunch, caught up and shared our caregiver woes, some similar and some very different. Every night, when things would finally settle down at home, I'd look forward to making my plays in my four or so games with Annie, either in the dark of my mom's room as I watched over her, or in my own bed just before falling asleep.

A few weeks ago, I was super busy with watering the gardens, friends visiting, getting out for a rare hike in the gorge... and in the back of my mind I kept thinking that I hadn't seen Annie make a play for several days. When things calmed down, I checked her Facebook page and found that what I feared was true. Annie's mom had died.

Immediately I began to cry really hard... for Annie, and for me, too. It was one of those rare times, during the hectic day-to-day business of this caregiving job, that I realized fully what is coming, and how completely unready for it I will always be.

I fled to the garden, unable to really see through the tears, and cut all my favorite hydrangeas for Annie; this was the most important step I could take at that moment. I called her later and heard some of her story, feeling new pain because I knew that many of the symptoms her mom had to endure, my mom has also.

The next day, I left the flowers on her porch. She wrote and told me that the hardest time is waking up in the morning, and so she has the hydrangeas by her bed so she will see them first thing, and remember that life goes on. A few days later, when I checked my Scrabble games, there was Annie, constant as the northern star.

~*June 2, 2012*

"Hydrangeas" illustration by Linda Santell

"*Your entire life journey ultimately consists of the step you are taking at this moment. There is always only this one step, and so you give it your fullest attention. This doesn't mean you don't know where you are going; it just means this step is primary, the destination secondary. And what you encounter at your destination once you get there depends on the quality of this one step.*" ~ECKHART TOLLE

CELEBRATING *the* LIFE *of*

Ruthe Ballard Figart Sphar

JANUARY 6, 1931–JULY 24, 2012

Funeral program cover design by Trish Noe. This essay was the program's insert.

summer

Let's roll: A tribute to Ruthe

My God and I go in the field together; we walk and talk as good friends should and do.
We clasp our hands, our voices ring with laughter; my God and I walk through the meadow's hue.

~GEORGE BEVERLY SHEA, FROM *MY GOD AND I*

My mother did not want it said that she died peacefully. True, she was in her home, surrounded by the people and things she loved. But despite the fact that she had no fear of making the transition out of her earthly, physical form, she fought willfully for more time here, mainly to be with me, her only child.

In life, however, she was a peacemaker, helping dissenting parties to focus on common ground long enough to realize the folly of their conflict. She was a teacher, a student, a leader, a speaker, a writer, a decorator, an accountant, a musician, a nature enthusiast, an animal lover, a baseball fan, a fashion maven (she could tell you exactly what she wore at every important event of her life)—and a spirited woman who wholeheartedly supported her family and partners, while paradoxically remaining staunchly independent.

The third of four daughters born to a farming couple in Clark County in 1931, Mom gleaned her sense of fashion from her father, who wanted his girls stylishly clad, even during the Depression. If growing up with few possessions created in the sisters a penchant for the finer things, they were nonetheless well aware that spirituality trumped materialism every time.

Losing her mother at age 16 must have contributed to Ruthe's early individualism and maturity. Georgetown College student Ross Figart was the visiting youth minister at Carlisle Baptist Church the summer of 1948 and he couldn't help but become fascinated with the most beautiful and interesting girl in the choir. Some of her favorite memories are of staying in the original Rucker Hall at Georgetown during their courtship. They were married in 1950.

My parents had been pastoring the county seat church in Vanceburg in Lewis County, Kentucky, for seven years when I arrived in 1964; Mom nearly died having me and doctors cautioned, "Don't try this again." Not one to gravitate toward anyone else's children, she loved her only child fiercely and spared no energy in teaching me her spiritual values, her thirst for great literature and music, and her love of all creation, especially birds and cats. My earliest memories are of her scrubbing coal dust off of me and off our black and white tomcat in Hazard, Kentucky, where she would emerge from our tiny mountain parsonage ready for church looking like a combination of Donna Reed and Jackie Onassis.

Throughout my life, I've been told by Kentuckians of all ages how much my parents influenced their spiritual development. During my dad's 13 years as director of missions for Boone's Creek Association, and his 11 years as director of missions for the Kentucky Baptist Convention, I watched my mom live her roles of "preacher's wife" and "missionary's wife" to their fullest— from the slate-rock hills of Eastern Kentucky to the jagged coastline of Brazil, South America. She had a gift for helping others to reach their potential, whatever the field of interest.

Growing up in the idyllic setting of Boone's Creek Camp, I tagged along as Mom led campers on nature hikes and bird walks through the wooded hillsides. I watched her transform the tiny timid Corinth Church choir into a forceful ensemble that could deliver a cantata to rival those she'd been a part of during music weeks at Ridgecrest Conference Center in North Carolina. Sometimes we'd arrive at a church where Dad was slated to interim preach, and when

Ruthe collage by Trish Noe

no one came forth to play the piano, Mom would matter-of-factly assume the bench, unrehearsed and unruffled.

Any time I heard her speak publically—from small circle gatherings to state WMU conventions—she always made herself vulnerable to her audience by sharing a moving anecdote or reciting a powerful verse that would inevitably bring my highly emotional "Mom Bit" to tears. But this caused others to respond on a far deeper level than would have been possible if she had refrained from crying.

After my dad died in 1992, Mom finally had her own college experience when she majored in English at the University of Kentucky in her mid sixties. She won awards for her writing, as her daughter had done decades earlier—not surprising since my communications talents were obviously inherited from her. She won an entire piano once for writing in 100 words, "Why I love my Baldwin." Never forgetting her Georgetown connection, she supported the school whenever possible as a way of honoring my dad.

When Mom fell in love with Bill Sphar in 1999, she cycled back to the farm life she had left behind in childhood. After five years of traveling and enjoying Spring Hill together, he became ill and she managed his daily care for two years. In the stressful throes of caregiving, she accidently ran over her own dear cat, Louisa, and a part of her soul never recovered from this trauma. Her strength and determination made Bill's final transition a comfortable one. When she left the farm, she took with her his faithful hound, Bebe, and gave her a life of luxury until her death this past January.

When Mom could no longer continue teaching her beloved adult Sunday School class at First Baptist Church in Winchester, she turned her creative energies to writing a memoir of her bucolic childhood, *A Feast for Charlie*, which was published earlier this year. About the same time, God sent Paula Underwood Rhodus—who was born and raised in Vanceburg a decade after we left—to help me care for my mother. Every day Paula came, Ruthe taught her something new—about birds, about flowers, about language, about music, and about life. Paula gave Mom a new connection to one of her favorite communities and provided an opportunity for her to continue to teach at home.

Ruthe never lost her sharp mind, offbeat sense of humor or "the-show-must-go-on" poise. Whenever she became bored with crossword puzzles and Neiman Marcus catalogs, Mom would gaze resolutely at me or Paula and say, "Let's roll." We'd get her into the small transport chair and she would pedal along as we rolled around the house—first to the screened-in back porch to see her squirrels, rabbits, finches, woodpeckers, hummingbirds, cardinals, wrens and blue jays; her roses, crepe myrtles, hydrangeas, herbs and tomatoes on the vine. Next she'd visit favorite books in the library, gleefully wake the cats from their naps, watch fervently from the front door as we went to retrieve her abundant mail, and sometimes she would play hymns on her piano, as she always had, by ear.

On the night of July 23, 2012, Mom watched with satisfaction as the Reds trampled the Astros. As the game ended and we got ready to go to sleep, she looked at me on the couch beside her bed and said earnestly, "I love you too much." I responded, "And I you." After that, she closed those piercing eyes that remained ever clear and bright, and I imagine she must have said to her Lord something along the lines of, "Let's roll."

The Georgetown College flag was lowered to half-staff for two days after Ruthe's passing to honor her inimitable spirit. Her ashes were scattered in Lewis County, Kentucky's Kinniconick Creek. We will all miss her grace, humor, insight and unconditional love.

~August 9, 2012

"Timeless Ruthe at Piano" illustration by Linda Santell

# fall

Songs of a new order

I was not ever thus, nor prayed that Thou shouldst lead me on;
I loved to choose and see my path; but now, lead Thou me on.

~JOHN HENRY NEWMAN, FROM *LEAD, KINDLY LIGHT*

My mother gave me many gifts, one of the most treasured being the sensibility to appreciate the artistic marriage of music and words. Those who were able to attend her funeral heard an array of classical, traditional and contemporary compositions that were chosen and put in order by her—not recently, but years before she passed. She included on her program (which she helped to design and approved just before her death) the special lyrics above from a favored hymn, which continue: *I loved the garish day, and spite of fears, pride ruled my will. Remember not past years.*

Music became a part of my grieving and my mourning even during the long night spent clearing and cleaning immediately after Mother's body had been taken from our house. For several days I could only find solace in the offerings of Bruce Cockburn, a Canadian singer songwriter I've always loved for his ability to write about spiritual matters from a Christian foundation moderated by a cultural perspective that does not diminish others of the world's religions. It was my own choice to place some Cockburn lyrics on the back of Mother's program, words I had never understood until I listened to them during that long night after her death.

Something jeweled slips away
Round the next bend with a splash
Laughing at the hands I hold out
Only air within their grasp
All you can do is praise the razor
For the fineness of the slash

~BRUCE COCKBURN FROM *THE ROSE ABOVE THE SKY*

Some weeks ago, I was able to get out the tiny tape recorder that I kept near the piano for the times when Mom could sit there and allow some of her favorite pieces to fly from her weakened fingers. I listened one whole afternoon to the scattered recordings I'd made, remembering the joy that overwhelmed me each time I heard her play once again when I had begun to doubt she would make it back to the bench. On some of those occasions, she would play *My God and I,* which was sung by a friend at her service according to her plan.

A few weeks (maybe even a few days) before Mother passed away, she had just finished playing the piano when she asked me a painful question: "Do you think there is any way that I can possibly get better?" As I was trying to formulate my response, I thought immediately of Cindy Bullens and her CD *Somewhere Between Heaven and Earth.*

I don't remember how I learned of Bullens and the 1999 album of 10 songs she recorded as a tribute to her 11-year-old daughter who died of cancer—but the work has long been an inspiration. The genre is light progressive rock, influenced by the likes of Carol King, Joni Mitchell, Heart and the Indigo Girls. Lucinda Williams and Bonnie Raitt make small contributions to a couple of the songs. But it's the introspective lyrics in combination with the poignant melodies that give this work its ability to help anyone who is mourning. Bullens unabashedly carries the listener through the various stages of grief, with tangible examples like a trip to Paris seeming dull in comparison to memories of her daughter and the impossible hope that a scientific discovery like finding water on the moon can somehow mean young Jessie will find her way back to earth.

With Bullens and her acute loss in mind, my answer to my mother took the form of another question: "What if there was an 11-year-old child here, whom we loved, and who had cancer—and we knew she was going to die? What if she asked us this question? How could we answer her?" I then told my mom that it was time for her to practice what she preached, and to talk to God, in her own way, so that she could prepare for where she was going. I told her, in effect, to let go of the things of this world, and to begin to look forward to the next.

And now it is me who is left here trying to let go—of her. It's hard when your mom was cool, was someone you hung out with, loved the things you loved, understood human nature in all its flawed nuances and exercised her sharp language skills and dry sense of humor up until a few hours before she took her last breath. It's hard when you're a relentless perfectionist, constantly plagued with feelings that you could have done more, should have done better as a caregiver. It's hard living right where it all went down, the set and setting for our last two years together. And it's hard when a relatively non-material girl has an accumulation of 81 years of sentimentally charged high-caliber material possessions to sort through, deciding what to keep, and doling out the rest as best she can to those who will appreciate them as much as Ruthe did.

But one of the lessons I have learned from my grief is that if I can do some good now for others around me, then Mother lives on—because in some way I become her as I move forward.

And move forward I have decided to do. I have the beautiful house we shared in Winchester, Kentucky up for sale, and whether it sells in two weeks or two years, I am soon headed to the mountains of Western North Carolina to seek work and a new beginning. When my father was working at Ridgecrest Baptist Conference Center outside of Asheville the summer he was courting my mom, he took her on several memorable hikes; she even made it up the strenuous trail to Upper Catawba Falls, which is no small feat. They loved the mountain forests there—and so do I.

Another lesson I have learned from my grief is this: When someone dies, there is a shifting and a shuffling that happens in preparation for the "new order" left behind. To use a baseball analogy, when one player is out of the game, the lineup changes. Since losing Mom, I have gotten closer to some folks I'd never really known before, including some of her close friends and members of our extended family who've come forward to lend support. Even among my own close friends, the shifting and shuffling is apparent; new bonds are formed as everyone rallies to take a position that will not only offer me strength, but also allow for growth that somehow just wouldn't have been possible before.

True, like the protagonist in Gillian Welch's traditional-sounding song *Orphan Girl,* "I have no mother, no father, no sister, no brother"—but I feel more whole and connected each day, nonetheless. Some lyrics from Cindy Bullens express it best:

There's a curious freedom rising up from the dark
Some kind of strength I've never had
Though I'd trade it in a second just to have you back
I gotta try to make some good out of the bad
So I laugh louder
Cry harder

I take less time to make up my mind and I
Think smarter
Go slower
I know what I want and what I don't
And I'll be better than I've ever been
Better than I've ever been

~October 4, 2012

Afterword added August 2016:

When I was little, I loved the word "beast." I fell in love with it because once when I was about five, my mom called our cat, Kitty Bo, a "beast" when he came in all wet and she was drying him off. I said, "Don't call him something bad!" And mom said, "A beast is a good thing." So I said, "Okay, if it's good, then I am going to call you that!" From that point on, my mom and I always called each other Beast. One would call the other and say, "Beast!" really fast first thing on the phone; we did this our whole lives together.

When I think of my mother now, it is of her entire essence as a timeless soul that had a huge effect upon me and upon all with whom she came in contact, giving us a richer life because of the joy with which she embraced all living things. The illustration that graces this chapter is a whimsical way I envision her now, gracing and enchanting the beasts of the woods (including some cats) with her ethereal music.

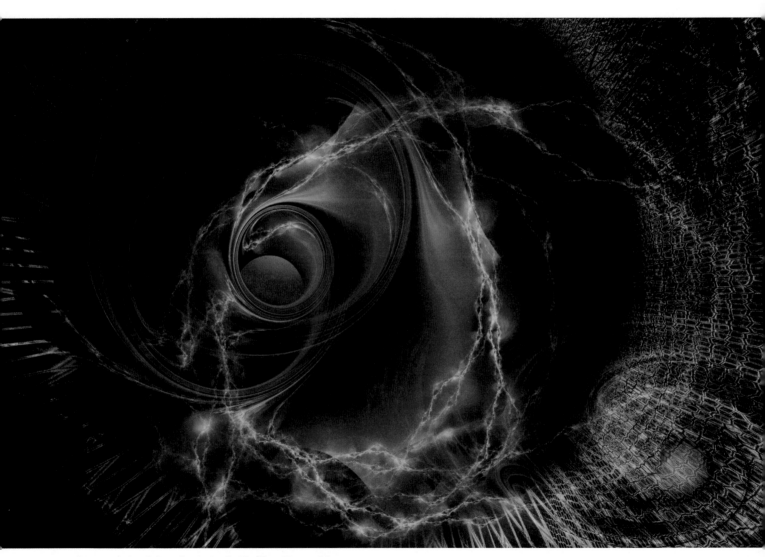

"Dragon's Lair" digital painting by Kathleen Farago May

winter

Changes are shifting outside the world

No more "I love you's"—the language is leaving me in silence
No more "I love you's"—changes are shifting outside the world*

~JOSEPH HUGHES AND DAVID FREEMAN

As a student of English Literature, I learned that for a narrative work of any kind to be truly engaging, the main character has to undergo a change.

In the terminology of dramatic structure, going all the way back to Aristotle, there is a climax or turning point that marks a change—for better or worse—in the protagonist's affairs. Consider the Shakespeare plays you recall: In the comedies, like *A Midsummer Night's Dream*, things had gone badly for the character up to this point, and now the tide will turn and things will get better. In the tragedies, like *Hamlet* or *Othello*, the opposite occurs, and events shift from good to bad at the climax.

Of course, by the time we learn about this literary device, we've already been exposed to it many times, from the earliest fairy tales and stories that were read to us as very young children on up through just about every form of entertainment that is a part of our particular age group's contemporary culture. We can all name our favorites: I recall being enchanted by *Alice in Wonderland*, *Treasure Island*, *Robinson Crusoe* and *Great Expectations*.

As adults, whether we love fiction, theater, opera or rock-n-roll, we are most inspired by those works of art in which a transformation occurs. I will find myself quite bored by films in which the main character never "gets it" and conversely reduced to tears by those in which the change the protagonist undergoes is portrayed in a startlingly realistic way. Some random examples of favorite films are *The Razor's Edge, The Darjeeling Limited*, Sally Potter's *Yes*, and most recently, *Last Cab to Darwin*. Similarly the music which affects me most profoundly—penned by artists like Joni Mitchell, Bruce Cockburn, James McMurtry, Jeff Tweedy, Steve Earle and Vic Chesnutt, just to name a few—does so through its ability to portray characters realizing something transformational.

Joseph Campbell took the Greek notion of dramatic structure a step further to define the common plot element in all stories as the hero's journey. In any narrative, things are going along routinely, and then the main character is faced with an upheaval of some kind in which all he thought was stable has now changed, requiring him to rise to the occasion and fight a dragon of some sort or another, usually representing a personal fear. It is through this battle that transformation occurs and the hero emerges a new, better, stronger person than before. Think *Wizard of Oz, Star Wars, Harry Potter, The Hobbit, Castaway, Avatar*, the list goes on and on.

I recently watched a film called *Finding Joe* that expounds Campbell's hero's journey concept. It does this through interviews with a dozen or so articulate speakers who have achieved greatness, some well known and others who worked quietly behind-the-scenes to accomplish successful projects. "Follow your bliss and the universe will open doors for you where there were only walls." This quote, which might as well be Campbell's tagline, is one of the main ideas behind this uplifting film, from which you'll come away feeling like an esteemed squad of cheerleaders including Deepak Chopra, Mick Fleetwood and Laird Hamilton is rooting for *you* personally.

But to witness another person taking on the ultimate hero's journey leaves us empty, mystified and lost—because when the final dragon is met and fought with, the essence of what the person was here in this realm of form actually seems to leave us, nevermore to return.

"The weakening or dissolution of form, whether through old age, illness, disability, loss, or some kind of personal tragedy, carries great potential for spiritual awakening— the dis-identification of consciousness from form. Since there is very little spiritual truth in our contemporary culture, not many people recognize this as an opportunity, and so when it happens to them or someone close to them, they think there is something dreadfully wrong, something that should not be happening." ~ECKHART TOLLE FROM *A NEW EARTH*

Trying to come to some terms with my mother's death over the past five months has been like trying to wake up after being heavily sedated. One is so overwhelmed with the grieving process that it's like being mired in physical, psychological and emotional quicksand. After many months of struggling just to get through each quagmire of a day, finally, strangely, you begin to process emotions and information like yourself again.

A few weeks ago, I was driving through the woods at sunset feeling as if I had been a victim of amnesia and was trying to remember something about who I had been before. It was like hearing snatches of a melody and parts of a lyric hovering just below the mind's surface, almost reachable and yet, still distant.

After chasing my ethereal thoughts for roughly a 24-hour period, a revelation of sorts began to emerge from the clouds, like mist rising from a mountain ridge. It was slowly dawning on me

"The Dream is Real" digital painting by Kathleen Farago May

that just because I can no longer see and hear and feel my mom doesn't mean she is not still on her journey.

Separate wholly from any learned connection between death and religion, the simple truth becoming less and less dim was that, given our limits of understanding, there is no reason to believe the changes do not go on. Changes are very likely still shifting outside the world as we know it. As Eckhart Tolle explains, during illness and finally in death, "what is lost on the level of form is gained on the level of essence."

●　　●　　●

The night my mother died, I awoke from a deep sleep having heard some sound in our shared room. When I reached her, she was unconscious but still living. And then I experienced something I never could have anticipated. Her essence, what some would call her spirit, left her body and very rapidly spread out around me with a palpable aliveness. It is impossible to describe this because I didn't see or hear it or even feel it. (I was actually quite devoid of emotion at the moment it occurred.) I simply experienced it. And when it was over, her body had become a shell, not unlike that of an insect. Her essence went on. It was tangibly not trapped in the shell, which had died.

From that point on, I knew that to honor my mother was no longer to look at or touch her body, for it was no longer her. And so I sat near the body for only a short time, and then left the room and did not watch when it was carried out of our house.

Mother had fought the ultimate dragon; she had faced her fear and gone through the consummate change. Or had she?

The way we experience time in this realm of form brings a horrible finality to this type of separation from someone we love. But, we need not lose interest in the plot as we might do when watching a movie where no transformation seems to be occurring. Change can still be going on—and who are we to say that it couldn't be? Maybe the essence that used to appear in the form of my mother finally found the doors where before there had been only walls. For all I know, Mom is now on some level of the hero's journey that is beyond my comprehension.

My continued closeness to her essence gives me the impression that changes are indeed shifting outside this world and that she is still learning, growing and changing as she has always done.

~January 9, 2013

*The title of this essay is an intentional misquote from the song No More I Love You's in which the lyric actually reads, "Changes are shifting outside the word." The Annie Lennox cover of the song written by Joseph Hughes and David Freeman provides the very personal aural backdrop against which the essay was conceived.

II

life beyond grieving

"Sacred Red Rocks" photo by Frances Figart

Last hike on Mountain Springs Road

Believe in a tree
Trees know what every Zen master needs to know

~LAURA NYRO FROM *TREES OF THE AGES*

"Look, Daddy, it's a natural tree tunnel," shrieked the six-year-old girl in delight.

From behind the wheel of the sky blue Valiant Station Wagon, Ross Figart clapped his strong, olive-colored hands together once and smiled his biggest, sweetest smile. This signified his approval of the moniker his daughter had coined for sections of curving mountain roads where the trees were so old and their branches so outstretched that they literally joined each other over the roadway, forming a canopy.

The diminutive child arched her back, lifted her pointed little chin, pushed her unruly camel-colored hair behind her elfin ears and breathlessly took in the overwhelming vision of deep green hues rushing by and encasing them in wonder.

"It's like a dream world," she cooed, peering out the window and into the shady branches as they careened past, hoping to glimpse at least one fairy.

The year was 1970 and the roads took us through the forested hills of Eastern Kentucky, where my father made his living as a Southern Baptist minister. He preached not hell and brimstone, but compassion and forgiveness. People adored him wherever he went, whether it was to Hyden or Hazard, Pikeville or Prestonsburg. And he adored the mountain people and their culture, a love he also instilled in me—along with his love of nature and of trees. The greatest gift he and my mother would give me was an idyllic childhood that could rival that of Wordsworth in the foothills of the Appalachian Mountains, on the wooded premises of a summer camp that was part of their ministry.

After I grew up and left Kentucky, whenever we would connect on the phone, I could hear Dad smiling as he'd say, "You'd like where I went today." He would have just returned home from a trip to some remote community like Whitesburg, Grayson, Pippa Passes, or Booger Branch (yes, this is an actual place). "There were lots of natural tree tunnels."

Thirty years later in 2000, eight years after my dad had passed on, I finally got an opportunity to realize a lifelong dream: I went on a quest to find some forested property to purchase in Eastern Kentucky. I will never forget the first time I ever drove down Mountain Springs Road in Estill County, in search of a remote cabin that was listed for sale in an area called Furnace.

My sidekick that day was my spiky-purple-haired New Yorker friend Cindi, who had implanted herself in Estill County a few years prior, and quite staunchly I might add. Even streetwise Cindi, who is rarely caught off guard, was taken somewhat aback when I began to shriek like a child at the amazing trees, whose branches bent and met as if in prayer over the winding gravel road. "These are the natural tree tunnels!" I screamed at her over the din of the Rav4's tires on the thick gravel.

The cabin itself was situated on a knoll that crowned six acres, two miles in at the head of this heavenly mountain "holler." The greater forest of which this small plot of land was part teemed with wildlife! To a wood spirit like me, the place was perfect. Tree-covered, rustic, comfortable, private (the nearest communities were all 30 minutes away) yet accessible (I could get to my office in Lexington in an hour)—and with a few improvements and embellishments, it became utterly and completely home. My plan, very simply, was to live out my life on Furnace Mountain.

But fate had other ideas. In a few short years, everything would change. And it all started because I loved—and lost—the trees.

About five years into my stay, much of the land around the cabin was unsustainably and mercilessly logged, the beautiful forest habitat ravaged by the largest and most ruthless equipment used in the state. Catalyzed by this catastrophe, which I worked for a year to try to prevent, changes would lead me to let go of the one thing I thought I'd always keep: I sold the cabin.

But letting go of what we can't imagine letting go of always leads to new adventures—to realities that before could have only seemed like dream worlds from a childhood fantasy. Before long, I would be riding through natural tree tunnels in the lush forests of Costa Rica. And from that land of diversity, I'd eventually return to Kentucky to help my mother die, two decades after losing my father.

As I write this, I'm getting ready to spend my last day as a Kentucky resident. Tomorrow I'll head south and try to make a new life for myself in Asheville, North Carolina. I'll be living at 3,000 feet elevation overlooking the city and surrounding Blue Ridge Mountains, with abundant bird life, resident white squirrels, black bears passing by and natural tree tunnels surrounding me once more.

Last week, I returned to Mountain Springs Road for a hike with my dear friend Jane, who now has a small cabin not far from my erstwhile home, which is well cared for by its new owners. Every bend in the two-mile road brought memories flooding back. We hiked on Forest Service Road 2057, which I used to walk with my dogs almost every day for the six years I lived there; I was walking on that road when the planes hit the towers. We visited the special rock sanctuary there, a sacred formation known only to a handful of locals. And I said my goodbyes.

I love Eastern Kentucky. And, although I'm not sure what is coming next, I cannot deny that I also love change—probably as much as I love mountains, mountain people, and trees. North Carolina, ready or not, here I come.

~April 13, 2013

"Mood Over Asheville" photo by Joe Lamirand

Fifties,

here I come: Eleven lessons from my forties

*"If you no longer want to create pain for yourself and others…
then don't create any more time."* ~ECKHART TOLLE

Tomorrow I turn 50. This afternoon I got a birthday message from Laura, a younger friend I met in Switzerland around the time I turned 40. Over the years I've known her, Laura has had many ups and downs and now has created a successful culinary business for herself on a Swiss farm. We have only been together twice, but shared a deep connection and enjoyed comparing notes about how to deal with life's challenges. After an initial greeting, her opening words were these:

"I often think about you and imagine you are happy. 50 now… I remember last time when you were 40. Loads of questions and thoughts about life: How is it today? How did these past 10 years help you find peace and answers?"

Wow! These immense, broad questions came to me at just the right moment, as I'd already been formulating the vague idea for a blog to reflect on the past decade in some comprehensive way.

My forties were incredible, and I migrated through many changes, the culmination of which was the death of my mom, and the realization that she was the true love of my life—even as I was flitting about on several continents during my stint in the travel industry. Finally going home to Kentucky to help her die was the best decision I ever made and, although I didn't do it perfectly, I was strong and I helped her live her last days the way she wanted to.

In 2013, I sold a house, moved, rented for six months, got a part-time job, and then bought a house and renovated it... all of which have led me to my current situation, a new resident of Asheville, NC, still recovering from loss, but growing stronger as I connect with my new community, and find my niche socially and professionally.

What follows is a collection of salient lessons from the past decade, each supported by a favorite quote.

LESSON 1: LOVE YOURSELF

"The most important relationship you have in life is the relationship you have with yourself."
~Diane von Furstenberg

Last year's birthday came at a time when I was still grieving the loss of my mom so heavily that I expected others in my life to somehow compensate for the internal void of having no parent left to celebrate my life in the way that only parents can. I learned then the final lesson of independence: that I really needed to only have expectations of my own self, and to face the fact that I was truly alone—and be okay with that. And that helped me to focus on my relationship with myself more in the past year than I ever had previously.

LESSON 2: LOVE OTHERS

"The beginning of love is to let those we love be perfectly themselves, and not to twist them to fit our own image. Otherwise we love only the reflection of ourselves we find in them."
~Thomas Merton

This is only common sense, but with those expectations mentioned in the first lesson always creeping into relationships, keeping the right attitude toward love of any kind can be a challenge. It's good to be reminded day after day that what we love about others is what makes them different from us and it is not our job to shape them or mold them into something we think is best for them—or for us. I think I finally learned this lesson during my forties and am ready to practice it well in the next decade.

LESSON 3: **ACCEPT WHAT IS**

"Stop resisting. So much of our anguish is created when we are in resistance. So much relief, release and change are possible when we accept, simply accept." ~Melody Beatty

During my forties, I think I adopted a more natural acceptance of reality, learning more about not pushing for things but allowing them to come to me organically. A huge lesson of grief is the acceptance that you cannot change what has happened, what is. Learning to relax into the "luxury of grief" and allow it to consume you for a period of time is actually healthy, and takes you on a tour through all of your emotions so that none is left unvisited—and then you are ready to move on, to move forward.

LESSON 4: **BE HERE NOW**

"If you no longer want to create pain for yourself and others... then don't create any more time... realize deeply that the present moment is all you ever have. Make the Now the primary focus of your life." ~Eckhart Tolle

I can't stress enough how much reading Eckhart Tolle helped to shape my outlook during my forties. It was like a homecoming finding his writing, because so much of what he says, I feel I've always operated on, and just thought that no one else was like me. These were lessons hard-learned and I made plenty of mistakes, but meditation and focusing on the Now helped me prepare to help my mom die, and live through it and on beyond it with a new enthusiasm for life.

"My Last Friday Morning" photo by Joe Lamirand

LESSON 5: BE STILL

"It is said that all you are seeking is also seeking you, that if you lie still, sit still, it will find you. It has been waiting for you for a long time. Once it is here, don't move away. Rest. See what happens next." ~Clarissa Pinkola Estes

As a natural progression of learning not to push so hard for what you want and to accept what is, there comes a realization that you are moving toward things as they are also moving toward you—that it's not up to you to facilitate getting there yourself; the movement is one greater than you can orchestrate. This doesn't mean do nothing; it means be open, listen and conserve energy in preparation for what is coming rather than spending it all. A great convergence is occurring and things are being worked out that you cannot imagine. So be still.

LESSON 6: BE IN NATURE

"I have passed the Rubicon of staying out. I have said to myself, that way is not homeward; I will wander further from what I have called my home—to the home which is forever inviting me. In such an hour the freedom of the woods is offered me, and the birds sing my dispensation. In dreams the links of life are united; we forget that our friends are dead; we know them as of old." ~Henry David Thoreau

Time in nature I always find to be my greatest teacher. Moving to Asheville was largely about connecting to natural areas and a sustainable lifestyle that values the environment. From my base in my new home here in the mountains, my intentions are set to contribute personally and professionally to the health of our natural resources, our true home. Through moving in this realm I know I will be comforted and cared for in many ways yet unforeseeable.

"To make the right choices in life, you have to get in touch with your soul. To do this, you need to experience solitude, which most people are afraid of, because in the silence you hear the truth and know the solutions." ~Deepak Chopra

I remember at a younger age feeling that for any experience to be truly meaningful, I had to share it with someone. As I've aged, I've become more and more comfortable with having amazing solo experiences, and enjoying them just for me, not even telling anyone about them. But this took a long time for me. As an only child, it was a hard lesson; I wanted to always be with others. This past year I've been alone more than ever before, and now I even have my own house. I confess I'm happier when others are visiting, but my alone time does provide many answers and insights. I feel I have more balance in this respect now than ever before.

LESSON 8: **GROW**

"No problem can be solved from the same level of consciousness that created it."~Albert Einstein

As we continue to evolve into higher consciousness and greater awareness, we find ourselves able to tackle challenges that previously seemed beyond our grasp. Lessons learned become the foundation for new ways of taking care of our self, interacting with others and moving through our sphere of existence. Suddenly some things that always seemed hard in the past are now parts of everyday life. This is growth.

LESSON 9: **EMBRACE SURPRISES**

Whenever I have extra time at my job at The Compleat Naturalist, I take a moment to read some of our wonderful children's books. Many of them remind me of the love of my parents, and none more so than *Wherever You Are, My Love Will Find You* by Nancy Tillman.

"Up in Rocky Fork" photo by Joye Ardyn Durham

I had thought that once I found romantic love again, I would be so sad that my new partner could not meet my parents or know them that it would make the relationship somehow impossible. But something happened that I could never have imagined.

I met someone who loves me in so much the same way that my parents did, that it is as if this person was sent to continue that deep connection—and that through him, their love has found me. So what I thought would be a desire for them to have met each other is transformed into a serendipitous feeling that they are the same energy, and know one another through understanding and loving me. This is a form of being surprised by joy that I could never have anticipated. I feel that all the other lessons somehow prepared me to be open for this one!

"So hold your head high and don't be afraid
To march in the front of your own parade
If you're still my small babe or you're all the way grown
My promise to you is you're never alone
You are my angel, my darling, my star
And my love will find you, wherever you are."

LESSON 10: KEEP MOVING FORWARD

"Inner strength comes only to those who move forward in the face of adversity."
~Phil Stutz & Barry Michels in "The Tools"

The Andean Torrent Duck spends its entire life swimming upstream against a strong current. You can see some cool video of it in the PBS nature movie *An Original Duckumentary*. This species—now in decline due to pollution, forest destruction and hydroelectric damming—really inspires me! No matter what your passion or intuition, it's all about picking a path and moving forward on it... whether you've got the perfect plan or not. Sometimes going out on a limb will create adverse situations, but learning to persevere through the storms will make us stronger—and help us appreciate the calmer days.

LESSON 11: DON'T FEAR MISTAKES

"I hope that in this year to come, you make mistakes. Because if you are making mistakes, then you are making new things, trying new things, learning, living, pushing yourself, changing yourself, changing your world. You're doing things you've never done before, and more importantly, you're doing something. So that's my wish for you, and all of us, and my wish for myself. Make new mistakes. Make glorious, amazing mistakes. Make mistakes nobody's ever made before. Don't freeze, don't stop, don't worry that it isn't good enough, or it isn't perfect, whatever it is: art, or love, or work or family or life. Whatever it is you're scared of doing, do it. Make your mistakes, next year and forever." ~Neil Gaiman

One of my closest girlfriends in my new town I met through my time in Costa Rica with Bruce Smith of Seascape Kayak Tours. Nina is a constant inspiration and has given me a great deal of emotional support in my new life here. She posted this quote before the dawn of 2014, but it is apt for the eve of a new decade for me as well. It sums up much of the feeling behind this essay, in that I intend it to be helpful to others, and in no way to say that I have not made tons of mistakes along the way. I have made them... and I encourage you to make them too. And then forgive yourself, and move forward.

Fifties, here I come.

~February 24, 2014

"All you are seeking is also seeking you…if you lie still…it will find you." ~CLARISSA PINKOLA ESTES

"The Summer Missionary" illustration by Linda Santell

The summer missionary and Ernie's salvation

What He says we will do
Where He sends we will go
Never fear, only trust and obey

~JOHN H. SAMMIS FROM *TRUST AND OBEY*

Legend has it that, as a child, I slept through a lot of my dad's sermons. In fact, I can remember doing this. I'd curl up beside my mom on the padded pew and drift off into the deep slumber of an active preacher's kid growing up at a camp, lulled by the rich and familiar tone of my dad's stentorian voice.

Even in my sleep I believe the structure of the sermons reached me on some level, as when I consider the way I construct my own essays today, I believe they are derived somewhat from the sermons my dad so eloquently delivered, speeches that were essentially essays themselves.

Dad had a great formula. He'd start on a personal level, relating an everyday down-to-earth anecdote to establish a bond with his listeners. Then he'd read a passage of scripture and do some analysis of it, bringing to bear on the text the words of contemporary scholars, professors and his own insights. To me as a child, this part seemed to go on and on.

But then came the part I liked best: some story or illustration that, at first, would seem completely out of the blue. When he'd start telling this story, some compelling, magical quality came into his voice that usually caused me to wake up to listen to it. I learned that the tale would have pertinence to the topic beyond all expectation. As the voice of Francis Ross Figart, Jr., built up into an insistent crescendo, it suddenly became clear to all that the point of this analogy was exactly what the scripture was saying.

I remember two such illustrations in particular: one about not judging and one about trust.

The first story was about how my dad went to the airport in Louisville in the late '60s to pick up a "summer missionary" from some other state who would be working with the small churches in Eastern Kentucky to help them run programs like Vacation Bible School. I think her plane was delayed and when he picked her up they basically had to drive directly to a church service up in the mountains.

When Dad met the young woman at the airport, he was startled to see that she was dressed impeccably from head to toe in an expensive white suit that was the fashion of the day. Dad worried on the way to the hollers whether this gal knew what she was getting into, and was concerned she might not be well suited to work with the people in the impoverished area they were driving to.

As they made their way up into the foothills of the Appalachians, it was evident that recent rains had brought flash flooding and creeks were running high. When they got to the small mountain mission, the people from the community were also arriving and several little children were playing in the churchyard.

Unlike the new summer missionary, these kids weren't wearing their Sunday best. Families in that area often did not have running water, kids were usually covered in coal dust, and in fact, Dad said, they had gotten pretty muddy playing on the soggy grounds of the tiny church.

Dad held his breath and watched as this woman who was dressed so impeccably got out of

"Ernie's Salvation"
illustration by
Linda Santell

the station wagon, and immediately went toward the little kids, getting down on her knees to greet them with hugs and smiles. They instantly loved her because she talked differently and was so beautiful and interesting. She paid not one bit of attention to her attire, nor did the kids, and she turned out to be the best person for the job he could have ever imagined.

The other story was set on the campus of Kentucky's Georgetown College, my dad's alma mater where he was number one dude on the debate team. One of his good friends was a fellow student who, if my memory serves, was named Ernie. The fact that Ernie was completely blind didn't prevent him from being totally self-sufficient. He walked all over campus by himself because he had learned where everything was; he didn't let his disability slow him down.

One fall, Dad had just arrived back on campus to go through registration for the new semester. He was walking out of the admissions building and looked across the quad and saw Ernie, striding rapidly as usual across the courtyard. At the same instant that he saw Ernie, Dad also noticed that during the summer break some construction had begun on the main campus thoroughfare: where normally there had been a sidewalk, now there was a gaping pit, taller than a person. Ernie was confidently pacing right toward that huge hole!

Ernie was pretty far across the campus, but my dad had this booming voice that those who knew him distinctly remember. He called out the command: "Ernie, STOP!" And as Dad's voice echoed across the quad, just one step before disaster, Ernie did. He recognized the deep voice of his friend, trusted it, and obeyed. Dad went running over to Ernie to explain, and the two had a good laugh.

● ● ●

Not long before my mom died, she and I talked about these illustrations and she remembered them too. Maybe she recalled the details a little differently than I do—and even knew the scripture that went with them—but that doesn't matter to me. What matters is, the messages behind these modern day parables got through—to both of us.

My turn to pull it all together.

One of the big reasons I came to Western North Carolina has to do with the adage of not judging a book by its cover. Here in Asheville, it's common to see stereotypes of dress defied; often the person in a crowd who most resembles a homeless vagrant may be the one who has the most money. Conversely, it's not unusual for those who appear in the most fashionable attire to be the nitty gritty, hard working volunteers who help needy animals and children with deep commitment. Grubby Appalachian Trail hikers walking into a mountain town may just as well be doctors or lawyers as students or "trustafarians." I love being in an area that attracts and supports this equalizing factor.

My dad would probably call it the voice of God, but I think of it as my intuition when something tells me I need to slow down lest I fail to notice a gaping hole in front of me. Whatever it is, when it says, "stop," I trust and stop. And when it says, "go," well, as Daddy would say, you better believe... I go!

Trusting that intuition once again as part of an almost two-year long transition to a new place and new life, I've become engaged to an amazing person who defies many stereotypes and possesses wisdom and balance that I haven't encountered for about 22 years.

~April 19, 2014

Dedicated to F. Ross Figart, Jr. (Sept. 30, 1926–April 10, 1992)

Grendel's story

And if the Babe is born a Boy, he's given to a Woman Old,
Who nails him down upon a rock, catches his shrieks in cups of gold.

~WILLIAM BLAKE

I was one of those English Lit students who actually liked *Beowulf*. I loved the alliteration, but I was also strangely sympathetic to the monster, Grendel, and tried to look at the situation from his perspective. He was a primal predator and he needed to eat. What better to lunch on than a bunch of drunken he-men acting like primordial heroes!

Later, when my mom went to college in her mid sixties and studied the Anglo-Saxon epic, she, too, liked Grendel. In fact, her best buddy in the class was a young football player who came in one day having just finished the reading assignment, and voiced the sad, sincere complaint, "They killed Grendel's *mom!*" She and I always laughed about that phrasing, the thought that Grendel had not just a mother, but a *mom.*

We were equally delighted by John Gardner's novel, *Grendel,* in which the monster tells his side of the story, one of isolation and, ultimately, nihilism. From Gardner's perspective, Grendel wanted to be heroic like the men he preyed upon, but because he had been exiled from society, his values were, of necessity, not human.

"The Rock Star"
portrait illustration
by Paul Ramey

57

In the year 2000, I adopted two littermate kittens that were found in an abandoned barn. The fluffy calico I dubbed Chickadee, and the beautiful classic black cat was named Grendel. He was shy, but loving, the kind of creature who accepts affection somewhat apologetically and often slinks away from too much human attention.

As a kitten, Grendel had a normal mewing voice. During his "teenage stage," he once stayed out in the woods on Mountain Springs Road for several days, perhaps undergoing some feline rite of passage. Upon his return, the guttural cry that emanated from his vocal chords seemed to herald some mysterious transformation into a semblance of his literary monster namesake. He now sounded like a combination of a Siamese with a sore throat and what mountain people call a "painther cat."

Grendel lived with Chickadee, Belial and Jimmy, in a timber framed shed on the property of my Kentucky cabin in the wilderness on Furnace Mountain, near the Red River Gorge. Belial and Jimmy were truly feral cats, and barely touchable, while Grendel and Chickadee were somewhat tame, but still held a distance from most people. They could all come and go as they pleased, and returned to the shed when their automatic feeder dispensed their food three times a day. Theirs was an idyllic life. I recall long walks along the forest service road near my house, trailed by two or three of the shed cats, meandering through the woods at their own leisurely pace. I loved them all, but felt the strongest connection to Grendel. He seemed a bit smarter and more refined than the others.

Changes came to Furnace Mountain in the form of unsustainable logging on adjacent properties. I sold the cabin in 2006 to live for a few years in a city—and the shed cats were not city material. So they went to live in the country with a friend, who eventually ended up taking them to Boones Creek Camp, where I had grown up in the tiny community of Trapp, near Winchester. Jimmy, who was the most skittish, vanished shortly after leaving the mountain. The other three settled into a mostly feral life, holing up like refugees in some abandoned buildings across the road from the camp, but visiting the parsonage and office for regular feedings on the porch of the house I had grown up in.

From early 2008 until the fall of 2010, I lived in Costa Rica and Canada working with a kayak tour operator. I thought of the cats many times, but was not in touch with anyone who knew how they were. Then I returned to Winchester, Kentucky to live with my mom, whose health

A few months later, mid June, I got a call from Angel. She said coyotes had been seen in the area, and she suspected they had gotten two of the cats, as she now only saw one of them.

was beginning to fail. With the stress of adjusting to being a caregiver, it honestly did not occur to me until February of 2012 that some of the shed cats might still be at the camp. I drove the 15 minutes out there one Sunday afternoon, and what I found amazed me. Grendel, Belial and Chickadee were all still alive and well, feasting regularly on the porch of the camp residence/office, and living across the road in the dilapidated remains of an old homestead. They looked great, and they knew me!

The next few months were hectic because by now, my mom was very ill and I was with her 'round-the-clock. But I would manage to bring a bag of food out to the camp once a month for Angel, the woman who now fed them. Angel had evidently been left instructions from the previous camp director, Jim Smith, in no uncertain terms: something to the effect of, "Whatever you do, do not ever abandon the responsibility of feeding these cats!"

A few months later, mid June, I got a call from Angel. She said coyotes had been seen in the area, and she suspected they had gotten two of the cats, as she now only saw one of them. "Who is left?" I inquired. It was Grendel.

*Oki and Grendel
photo by Frances
Figart*

I went to see him soon as I could get away for an hour, and he walked me all around the premises of his dwelling, making his raucous bellow all the while, as if in mourning for his lost mates. He was all alone now, like the beast in *Beowulf*. He would not let me touch him, but he seemed to enjoy my companionship.

Since Angel was now his feeder, I instructed her to catch him when possible, and bring him to me in Winchester, where I lived with my mom. I would take him to the vet, and if he checked out fine, I'd bring him into our home to be a companion for our kitten, Oki.

At first, Oki was incensed that another cat even existed, much less was in her home. But inside of two weeks, the two were cuddling and grooming one another. We had a monitor in my mom's room so we could hear her calling out when she needed something, and I recall hearing Grendel, over the roar of the oxygen machine, emitting his guttural roar as my dying mother tried to sleep. She asked me once, politely, "How long will Grendel be staying with us?"

Sadly for Mother, Grendel would be staying much longer than she could; she died in late July, only a month and a half after he arrived.

Nine months after Mom died, Grendel moved with Oki and me to North Carolina. The move was rough for him, and included an embarrassing stop at the Tennessee border to clean him up along the way. My friends Mary and Joe helped out, and when Grendel was ready to travel again, Joe said, in what has become an infamous metaphor, "Let's get this rock star to the show."

● ● ●

Now my family has gained three more beings: John (husband), Dukkha (Australian Shepherd) and Ivy (Mini Aussie). Grendel takes it all in stride. He is fully enjoying his retirement home on our six-acre homestead in East Tennessee, where he is finally free again to go outside whenever he pleases, but can also enjoy the cushy indoor environment at will. His interest in hunting long since diminished, Grendel mostly enjoys lounging in the sun on the huge rocks my husband designs into the landscape. While the little old feline still sometimes slinks away from affection, he seems more and more relaxed with each passing year, and always purrs when being carried or sleeping on my feet at night.

At the time of this printing, Grendel is almost 17 and is in great shape. Six years he was a shed cat on Mountain Springs Road, and six years he was feral and survived, thanks to Jim Smith and the camp Angels, and his own cat smarts. Who knows, perhaps six more years will have passed before we say goodbye again.

I know only this, that sometimes in the wee hours before dawn, he lifts up his raucous voice to the heavens and bellows out a sound that I'm sure would make even Beowulf wonder: *Is he giving thanks? Does he miss his mates from the old days? Does he want to prey on a mouse? Or does he just want more of his finely shredded cheddar cheese, NOW!*

~Originally penned November 8, 2014; final three paragraphs updated August 2016.

writing your future

"The Conductor" illustration by Linda Santell

Editors

Conductors of the publishing world

"I am that gadfly which God has attached to the state, all day long… arousing and persuading and reproaching… You will not easily find another like me."

~PLATO FROM HIS *APOLOGY*

I wrote this essay in March of 2013, during a time of traveling back and forth between Asheville, where I would soon be moving, and Winchester, Kentucky, where I was trying to sell the house I had shared with my mom and settling her estate. All the while, I was applying for jobs in the Asheville area. My goal was to find an editing gig. Around this same time, I began freelancing for The Laurel of Asheville.

I was recently asked by a potential employer to describe the editor's role within the publishing process. I immediately thought of Swiss conductor Mario Venzago, former Indianapolis Symphony Orchestra Music Director.

Each time I have attended a performance by a symphony orchestra, most memorably those directed by Venzago, I have sat through most of it in tears. Whether Bruckner or Wagner, Schubert or Liszt, Dvorák or Ravel, the music always moves me deeply. But the emotion comes more from the fact of identifying so strongly with the conductor, and seeing what he does as the quintessential metaphor for what I do, and what others do, when we are editors in every sense of the word.

We put it all together. We choose the material. We set the pace. We communicate and network with all the community stakeholders involved. We choose the players we feel can contribute the most effectively to our ensemble.

We coach others on minute details of their style and performance and somehow keep them feeling not criticized, but motivated because we are working together for something greater than us.

We hear and see the big picture of how everything needs to come together in the giant whole of a publication. And yet we orchestrate every single detail of everyone on the team pulling together to make it all happen as perfectly as possible.

We cross t's and dot i's a lot of the time. But we also plan, prod, goad, think at the 20,000-foot level so that others can focus on smaller parts, coach, mentor, teach, challenge others to reach their potential, juggle all the balls at once—all the while keeping time for the entire group.

Even now, having gone several years without seeing Venzago in action, without hearing the product of his amazing vision in the musical realm, I'm still stirred and motivated by remembering the times I was in his audience. And although he was released unexpectedly and inexplicably from his duties in Indianapolis, I know I join throngs of others in wishing him well as he continues to inspire those fortunate enough to see and hear him in Newcastle, Bern and beyond.

Not long after being asked to reflect on the editor's role, I attended a networking luncheon in Asheville, North Carolina. After everyone took turns delivering one-minute introductions, a woman came up to me and provided the name and e-mail address of someone she knew in publishing. "He might not be much help, though," she said. "He's just an editor."

Just an editor? *No,* I thought. No one is *just* an editor.

Our role is akin to that of Socrates, whom Plato described in his *Apology* as having said, "I am that gadfly which God has attached to the state, all day long... arousing and persuading and reproaching... You will not easily find another like me."

Perhaps like Mario Venzago, I continue to be amazed at our current economy and life's unexpected crescendos and diminuendos. But in the face of uncertainty, and when I wonder what comes next, I know one thing, and that is that I am proud to be an editor.

We are the conductors, the visionaries, the directors and the gracious gadflies of the publishing world.

~March 6, 2013

Paper dolls,
flow and the art of whatever!

Come, my friends. 'Tis not too late to seek a newer world.

~ALFRED LORD TENNYSON FROM *ULYSSES*

In his best-selling 1990 book, *Flow: The Psychology of Optimal Experience*, Dr. Mihaly Csikszentmihalyi (pronounced "chick-sent-me-high-ee") defined and explored the concept of "flow" as our experience of optimal fulfillment and engagement. He describes it as "a state of concentration or complete absorption with the activity at hand and the situation... a state in which people are so involved in an activity that nothing else seems to matter." Flow, whether in creative arts, athletic competition, engaging work or spiritual practice, is a deep and uniquely human motivation to excel, exceed and triumph over limitation.

Csikszentmihalyi gives me a form of self-confidence through his concept of "flow" that I confess I never gained from the term "art." As a society, we tend to think of "art" as primarily the creative arts—music, visual art forms and creative writing being the three that most readily come to mind. But those of us not blessed with talent in one of these areas are often left feeling like the ugly duckling or the Cinderella in a world full of artistically graced swans and stepsisters.

From childhood, I recall the many lessons (piano, ballet, tap, violin and voice) my mother

"My Favorite Paper Dolls"
illustration by Linda Santell

69

was enterprising enough to involve me in—all of which gave me my true appreciation for music, but none of which "stuck" in the sense that I ever felt from them "optimal fulfillment and engagement." Instead, I felt sick on the curvy roads to and from the lessons, mortal fear at recitals, self-consciousness about my too-thin body at dance reviews, and basically overwhelmed by what I call the perfectionist's script for self-defeat: with so many things to do, how could I ever do any one thing well?

To escape from the pressure, I'd retreat to my bedroom where hundreds of paper dolls waited to come to life under my direction. Silly as it sounds, for an only child with a vivid imagination, the world of girls and boys cut out from *Simplicity* magazine—evenly matched in size and each with his or her own intricately developed emotional and psychological makeup, set of academic skills, and personal history—was the key to power. This game cast me as the director, organizer and creator. I set up detailed schedules for each person and then watched with glee as my random schedule-making schemes placed Janice in a science class with Tom, a boy she had a crush on, or Jeff in choir with Candy, a girl he had broken up with and no longer wished to see. Aside from the social element, in the pretend world I created, these "students" gained skills that helped them determine their future careers; they made friends who would be with them for life, and siblings supported each other through difficult family issues. So empowering was this "flow" that I played with these dolls long past the "appropriate" age, and can vividly recall nervously throwing the covers down to hide all my dolls in their classrooms (individual squares on a quilt, actually) when my father unexpectedly knocked on my door when I stayed home from school with a cold as a high school freshman.

That very year, another form of flow superseded that of the dolls. My English teacher, Debby Douglas, was handing me back my umpteenth paper marked with an A++ and she must have seen something in my face that betrayed a certain disappointment and realized that I needed encouragement that defied expectation; I was used to getting these A's no matter what I did. "Other students get A's," she said, "but you need to understand that what you do is in a whole other category: this is something you do like no one else. You should really pursue it." From that moment on, I had my flow. I knew where I wanted to go, what I wanted to do—the world revolved around words, writing, communication: *that* was my music, *my* "art."

And yet, still that word "art" did it's best to make me feel left out. Because, save for bad lyrics written during some romantic squabble, I was never a creative writer. In college, I won contests for critical/analytical essays dissecting the language of Spencer and Shakespeare poems, short stories by Hemingway—even the lyrics of songs by Joni Mitchell. I was a nerdy writer, while those around me were poets, painters and potters, violinists, vocalists and artistic visionaries.

And then one day, years later, when I had my own business as a freelance writer, I decided to face the challenge. I knew I'd envied my friends who were musicians and artists too long. But why? Was it because I had not yet found that "deep and uniquely human motivation to excel, exceed and triumph over limitation"? "What is *my* art?" I asked myself. What is it that truly puts me into the world of "flow"? My writing did it, yes. But often, in order to make a buck, I was forced to write about topics for which I held no real passion. So what was my passion? How could I make a difference?

It was then that I remembered the paper dolls. And through a good, hard look at the nature of that experience, I realized that I had not just been playing a game; I'd been grooming myself, teaching myself, preparing myself for my future contributions to the world. My true gift was bringing people together, connecting and directing them to do great things, allowing them to support one another, and providing them a means to learn their true callings.

This realization took a shape that rapidly sprung to life in the form of a non-profit organization, Greater Opportunities for Women, to help low-income women in Kentucky learn about their talents and develop better job skills while supporting one another in a group, attending classes together for ten weeks. While developing and implementing this complex program, I felt like "an artist" in the truest sense, staying up all night in a rush of inspiration to finish creating an aspect of this intricately detailed work. I was like the conductor of a symphony, directing a team of volunteers to work together to pull off complex pieces of the "music" that I could not perform alone. It was near the end of my four-year endeavor with GO Women that my dear friend Paul Ramey pointed out that unlike that of a writer, musician or visual artist, my social form of art was *four*-dimensional because it touched the realm of possibility and actualized people to realize their dreams.

Once when one of the 60 women who attended the program decided to drop out, my mother remarked, "Unlike the paper dolls, GO Women don't always stay where you put them." Always perceptive, my mother hit the nail on the head with this statement. And ultimately, control freak that I was, perhaps that's why I eventually handed the executive director role off to someone else. Perhaps I just couldn't maintain that level of artistic intensity for longer than four years; after all, artists have their "periods." But I probably learned more from the adventure than anyone else; I learned that art, for me, is whatever gets me "in the flow," whatever challenges me to go beyond my limits, and to excel and triumph in new ways.

Today I have the privilege to work in publishing, bringing my writing, editing and organizational skills to bear on a unique and successful magazine. I feel that familiar sense of optimal fulfillment and engagement when I am planning all the articles that will go into an issue, organizing materials for a story, writing e-mails to sources explaining the kind of quote I need from them, instructing other editors, coaching new writers, or proofreading a magazine to ensure it is as error-free as possible. I love working with words, I always have. But it's the people part of my job as an editor that brings into play that fourth dimension of actuality that I learned and practiced in the time of playing with the paper dolls. I coach and direct a large group of writers, photographers and illustrators, and I work with another large network of community leaders to get their stories out to the public—and this is what gets me in Csikszentmihalyi's flow. *This* is *my* art.

"Come, my friends. 'Tis not too late to seek a newer world." These words from Tennyson's *Ulysses*, some of the few that stick in memory from my studies in English Literature, continue to send chills up my spine each time I hear them. Just as Ulysses rallied around him his old sailing buddies to go upon a new, and perhaps final, quest, we are never too old to set out on a new voyage, and see the world in a different way than we ever could before.

We all have to challenge ourselves to go beyond our limits—limits we have largely, though often unwittingly, set for ourselves. Whatever challenges you, whatever you wish that you could do, but fear you can't—I encourage you to give it a try. You might just become a new kind of artist—with a whole new sense of flow.

~ Originally composed in 2008, revised and published on my blog November 7, 2014; last three paragraphs updated July 30, 2016

The lights begin to twinkle from the rocks:
The long day wanes: the slow moon climbs: the deep
Moans round with many voices. Come, my friends,
'Tis not too late to seek a newer world."

~ALFRED, LORD TENNYSON, FROM *ULYSSES*

"Kurt Vonnegut Mural" photo by Warren Lynn

Intention,

practice and writing your own future

"You want to change the world? Change your thoughts!"

~KURT VONNEGUT

I once heard Kurt Vonnegut deliver an absolutely riveting talk. At its climactic crescendo he exclaimed, "You want to know the future? Just wait around for about five seconds. It's happening right now. You are creating it through your every thought and intention. You want to change the world? Change your thoughts!"

I remember including this and several other kernels of Vonnegut-inspired wisdom in a presentation I gave to various writers' groups in Kentucky. One was: "Not sure you're a writer? Check and see if you're writing." In other words, aptitude alone doesn't make you a writer; you need to make writing a daily practice.

About five years ago, a fork in my life's path could have easily swayed me from that practice. But I chose instead to use the circumstance to deepen it... and to add a new element to my writing: intention.

In October of 2010, I had just stepped away from an adventurous career in Costa Rica to spend time with my mom in Kentucky. I knew that I would be staying with her for the rest of her life. As the marketing and communications director for a kayak ecotour operation, I had been immersed in writing every day—handling all company communications and maintaining the web site and social media program I had created.

Rather than set aside the practice of writing each day, I started a blog.

●　　●　　●

Any body of work starts with a consideration of its audience. Even if we don't realize it, the person or group for whom an article, essay, poem or book is written is with us on a subconscious level. Sometimes we know the audience, and sometimes we write to attract an audience not yet within our sphere.

I started my blog with two audiences in mind: one general, and one very specific.

First, I wanted to keep my broad network of travel industry contacts abreast of what I was doing and to express myself personally and professionally to that global audience, which included members of The International Ecotourism Society, Sustainable Travel International and the Adventure Travel Trade Association.

Another, as yet invisible, audience was more specific: I was writing to an unseen publisher who would someday discover my work through taking the time to read this collection of reflective essays (as well as the parts of my blog that are a virtual résumé) and deem me worthy of investing in as a writer, editor and leader. This person would not just think that I was good, but would completely "get" me and fully recognize and utilize my potential to take a product or company to the next level.

I was setting an intention with the blog site. While I was putting my career on hold in order to care for my mother, I was at the same time creating a way to continually demonstrate my abilities by writing about my current role as a caregiver.

Many lessons were learned and incredible growth took place in the fertile ground of my commitment—though I felt hopelessly unqualified—to help my mother die and then manage her estate. I didn't do it perfectly, nor did she. It was hard, we were awkward, but we muddled through. While I could never master patience while she was here, once she was gone, miraculously, I had somehow become a much more patient person. All along the way, I wrote about the experience. Four of my best essays came to be penned throughout four difficult seasons: the spring of my mother's last days; the summer of her passing; the fall consumed by the luxury of grief; and the winter when I finally understood... she wasn't really *gone* at all!

That last essay, *Changes are shifting outside the world*, tells what it was like for me to be with my mother during her transition. It concludes thus: "The way we experience time in this realm of form brings a horrible finality to this type of separation from someone we love. But, we need not lose interest in the plot as we might do when watching a movie where no transformation seems to be occurring. Change can still be going on—and who are we to say that it couldn't be? For all I know, Mom is now on some level of the hero's journey that is beyond my comprehension. My continued closeness to her essence gives me the impression that changes are indeed shifting outside this world and that she is still learning, growing and changing as she has always done."

●　　●　　●

It's good to have intentions. What is sometimes hard is waiting for the time to be right.

A year later, I had relocated to Asheville, North Carolina, and was trying to find a job in which I could use my writing. On the morning of February 1, 2014, my blog received the following comment on the essay *Changes are shifting outside the world*.

"Beautifully stated! Your heart was opening to a wonderful knowing, love transcends all that is.... Peace of mind only comes through the heart and is felt sometimes long before it is known. I am happy for your knowing so thoughtfully expressed."

As I read that response to my writing, I knew that my intention was now actualized. I had

found my publisher.

And so, largely because of the events that have transpired through the act of visioning and creating my own future, I now have the great privilege to work as a magazine editor once again. It is my J.O.B. (joy of being) to direct *The Laurel of Asheville*, a decade-old, well respected monthly magazine showcasing the arts and culture of Western North Carolina.

What started as a blog in 2010 has now become this book. It took me four years to realize that those four essays penned during the four seasons of the year of my mother's transition were the groundwork for this collection of essays.

My audience has multiplied since my move to the Asheville area. So I write this to all my new friends, as well as all my long-time friends everywhere. I also write this essay for and dedicate it in utter thankfulness and humble appreciation to my very specific audience: *To Jerry, who took the time to read, to see, and to believe.*

~December 25, 2015

"Old Wooden Boat" photo by Warren Lynn

Epiphany

of a normal day: Keep being you

"One day I shall dig my fingers into the earth, or bury my face in the pillow, or raise my hands to the sky, and want, more than all the world, your return."

~MARY JEAN IRION

On this Twelfth Night, eve of Epiphany, when my mother would have turned 85, I reflect on the fact that many of the people I am closest to today—both geographically and emotionally—I did not even know five years ago in January of 2011.

At that time, I was in Kentucky, and suffering terribly because of a breakup a few months before that had left me feeling completely ungrounded. I had temporarily lost my identity in another, one with whom I finally had to sever ties in order to regain my self. I remember sobbing in my friend Candace's bedroom, "I've had to break up with Bruce, and I've realized I am at ground zero. I have no idea who I am!"

During my time of healing, I sought counseling and found, through a trusted friend's recommendation, a wonderful therapist who I will call Ryman. I saw him only five or six times, and I shared my story and brought him texts that I wanted to use to help me weather the storm until I found dry land again. They were passages from Eckhart Tolle's *The Power of Now* and Melody Beatty's *The Language of Letting Go*. Ryman and I made recordings of his voice and my own that I would play in solitude, reminding myself how to get back to center, where I needed to be.

The imagery of oceans, beaches, boating and water I closely associate with the time I spent in Costa Rica and Canada, supporting the small kayak ecotourism operation that belonged to my erstwhile lover and companion, Bruce Smith. I wanted this person to be the love of my life, but that was wishful thinking. Good to the environment and his clients, Bruce had a harder time being an anchor for those closest to him.

During the three- or five-day kayak trips he guided, Bruce would paddle in to shore from a remote island and I would meet him at the ocean's edge to replenish the supplies for his group. This scenario figured prominently in my therapy with Ryman. We created a visual meditation accompanied by vocal guidance to help me accept that helping Bruce would no longer be my role and that I needed to say goodbye to this man and his business for my own wellbeing. While Ryman's southern accent set the stage on a digital recording, I would visualize taking the supplies to Bruce, meeting him at the sea's edge, saying goodbye, and watching him paddle out and around the edge of the cove until he was no longer visible, knowing I would never go back there and do this again. Ryman's voice reassured me that this was right and okay and that I would survive it and be stronger in the end.

Ryman was a huge help in keeping me on course, though he constantly told me that I was the one steering the boat of my recovery—I was doing all the work, and he was just there to watch and listen. Months passed. I reached the shore of non-codependence and regained myself... just in time to be "of some comfort" to my mom in her final months.

●   ●   ●

Now, working in the Asheville area and living just north of town in East Tennessee, I have a whole new social pathway, but I keep in touch with many friends and acquaintances in Kentucky and the world over. I reach out to Ryman about once a year, and he always sends a

"Buoy Art" photo by Warren Lynn

message back to tell me a bit about his life. During the Twelve Days of Christmas leading up to Epiphany this year, I wrote a note to him, and his response left me reeling. Unbeknownst to me, during January last year he lost his wife, his lifelong soul mate, to a sudden illness.

"It has been a year filled with sadness, joy, thanksgiving, longing, some despair, etc., all fine and part of the process," he wrote. "Your experience after your Mom passed was part of a continuing reminder for me that [my wife] is alive and well in my heart and in every part of my existence and everything around me."

I responded: "I can tell between the lines that you are allowing yourself the privilege to be fully immersed in 'the luxury of grief,' which is a very individual experience, as unique as your relationship was. I can say nothing that will help, but only to allow all this to flow over you and into you like a river, without trying to map its course. I feel that at the 3.5-year point since I lost my mother, I am actually done with grieving because I have always allowed the grief to overtake me fully and take me wherever it wanted me to go."

I thought about what it really was that helped me get through the first year after my mom's death. I remembered that I felt the most lost and bewildered on the first Mother's Day (which was almost a year after she passed). I had relocated to Asheville, but knew only a handful of people and spent most of my time in solitude. I wished more than anything to be able to be counseled by Ryman at that time, but I was far away and alone.

"I read a lot of things but really, what's helped me most was just listening to my own heart and staying tuned in to my mother through common friends and through my writing about my grief," I wrote him. "Something that helps me that I've never really tried to write down is the notion of how we experience time as linear, when truly it isn't. Because of that, it seems that one person has to 'go' before another, but actually, we are all already everywhere together at once. During this horrible time of separation, you are forced to remain in this linear time illusion, while she is actually free of it. So as much as you can join her in that knowing that you are truly still together, the more free you become."

Ryman responded the next day: "I just read your email and thanks so much. I made a copy to keep in front of me as a reminder about getting centered with this experience. Today, I have been sad and had moments of feeling sorry for myself. It's of course all okay, but I want 'to allow it to flow over me and into me like a river' and be open to creating something new and different. I love your 'linear time illusion,' which nails the reality, leading me to say, 'Oh, I forgot about that!' Thank you for reminding me!"

●　　●　　●

I'm overjoyed that I could be of some help to this person who helped me remember who I was at a crucial time of self-doubt.

Even though now I am so much happier and centered than I was five years ago, I still have days of frustration and need reassurance. On one of these, recently, I received a message from a new colleague who texted me:

"Just keep being you: dedicated, visionary, warm, professional, deeply caring, funny, experienced, creative, kind, with a smile and laugh and deep heart that naturally just draws you in. What struck me when I first met you, then played out deeper as we started to work together, is that you do all these things with poise and class. Keep being you..."

One of the coolest things about that message was that while I read it, I felt somehow disoriented and seemed to travel back in time. For an instant, I thought I was reading a description written long ago about my mom—but then I realized, this was about me.

When I start to take any aspect of life for granted, I want to always remember Ryman and how, when I was stranded, he helped me get back in my boat and get back to shore in late 2010 and early 2011. I want to remember how sudden was his loss and how effervescent his ongoing resilience. I also want always to remember being with my mother in her last days and hearing her say, "I would give anything if I could just get out of bed and come to greet you when you get home from the grocery."

* * *

A message came to me today from someone I don't even know, as part of a chain of uplifting quotes:

"Normal day, let me be aware of the treasure you are.
Let me learn from you, love you, savor you, bless you, before you depart.
Let me not pass you by in quest of some rare and perfect tomorrow.
Let me hold you while I may, for it will not always be so.
One day I shall dig my fingers into the earth, or bury my face in the pillow, or raise my hands to the sky, and want, more than all the world, your return."
~Mary Jean Irion

~January 6, 2016

Afterword:

My latest correspondence from Ryman arrived in my inbox just before I finished editing this book in July of 2016. It included these words:

"I want you to know you are one of my heroes. I have seldom met a person who embodies the energy, passion and commitment to embracing life and striving to contribute and enhance the quality of your own life and anyone else who enters your world. I believe you recognize the potential of the human spirit and do everything you can to engage life with the determination

to live that potential. Thank you for being a model for all of us who know you."

Once again, this sounds like something that would have been written to one of my parents, not to me. I share it not from some illusion that I have any special gift, but from an understanding that, if I can be a hero, then anyone can! I, who felt the most inadequate that anyone could ever be during the entire time I was a caregiver, know now that there is no right way to do it; the one and only way is to just be there... and love.

Although I didn't do the job as well as I would have liked, and I still have sad memories of the moments when I lost patience, accompanying my mother through her transition taught me everything I know today about truly being alive. We can all practice letting go of the false notion that we are in control, stepping out of the clutches of time (the imaginary jaws of life) and being present for those around us in a way that helps us reach ever higher towards our true human nature—being just who we are... in the now.

There's a curious freedom rising up from the dark
Some kind of strength I've never had
Though I'd trade it in a second just to have you back
I gotta try to make some good out of the bad
So I laugh louder
Cry harder
I take less time to make up my mind and I
Think smarter
Go slower
I know what I want and what I don't
And I'll be better than I've ever been
Better than I've ever been

About the artists

Graphic designer **Trish Griffin Noe** is an award-winning visual communicator based in Lexington, Kentucky. She founded Noe Design in 1998 after a decade of design experience in publishing, advertising and marketing. She and Frances worked together briefly at a design firm in the early '90s, and she has remained the author's 'designer of choice' since. Her work includes corporate identity, branding, stationery systems, packaging, websites, newsletters and other publications. She designed Ruthe Sphar's book *A Feast For Charlie* as well as her funeral program. Trish spent many hours sitting with Ruthe during her final months.

The cover art is by **Joye Ardyn Durham**, who grew up in Harlan, Kentucky, where her parents knew Ross and Ruthe Figart. Now living in Western North Carolina, Joye is known for her landscape, nature and canine photographs and owns the Gingko Tree Gallery and frame shop in Black Mountain. She met the author through working as the lead contributor of photography for the quarterly magazine *Plough to Pantry*, which Frances edited. Her work has also been published in local publications such as *The Laurel of Asheville*, *WNC Magazine*, *Our State* and *Blue Ridge Travel* as well as in the *Wall Street Journal* and by Paramount Pictures.

Featured illustrator **Linda Santell** uses her talent to support projects that promote the well being of others and the planet. The inspiration for her images and fabric designs comes from the diverse harvest of local farms, her herb garden and other natural forms. Originally from Ohio, she lives in the historic district of Reidsville in Rockingham County, North Carolina. Her artistic contributions to the magazine *Plough to Pantry* sparked her inspired creative involvement with Frances and this book.

Photographer, musician and historic renovation artist **Joe Lamirand** was a good friend of Ruthe Sphar and helped to run her household in her final months. Joe is a film director, writer and producer known for *Talent, Hollow* and *Turning Japanese*, which won 'best short' at Cannes' American Pavilion Emerging Filmmaker Showcase. This book is dedicated to Joe, who became a close friend of the author in the early 2000s in Indianapolis, and his now-partner Mary, her childhood comrade. The two connected through caring for Ruthe, and when she died, the line-up changed.

Artist, writer and musician **Paul Ramey** works as graphic designer at OneBlood, a Florida-based blood collection agency. Paul is the author of the young adult historical mystery novel *Edgar Wilde and the Lost Grimoire*, artist/author of *Zen Salvador* (a limited-edition "art" book of dog wisdom dedicated to Salvador, his departed canine companion of 16 years), and composer/performer/producer of the 2-CD goth/rock opera *Veil & Subdue—The Courtship of The Black Sultan*. Paul first met the author in 1993, and through the years the two have enjoyed long arcs of deep and meaningful friendship and life exploration.

Photographer Warren Lynn is an ordained clergy-person within the Christian Church and serves as executive minister for Christian Vocations at Disciples Home Missions in Indianapolis. His passion for spiritual practice includes playing the Native American style flute, mindfulness meditation and walking labyrinths; he holds advanced certification as a labyrinth facilitator. Warren enjoys sea kayaking, and met Frances at Seascape Kayak Tours in New Brunswick.

Digital artist Kathleen Farago May grew up with the disparate influences of Budapest and Montreal woven through her childhood. The evolution from drawing to painting, to printing (etchings and silkscreens) and finally to digital painting has allowed an ever more clear expression of the spiritual impulses that drive her creative work. Kathleen and the author have never met personally, but know each other 'virtually' online through a mutual friend.

If you would like to share a copy of this book with someone,
links to booksellers can be found at francesfigart.com.

Made in the USA
Monee, IL
07 November 2020